THE MALADY OF THE CENTURY

FUTUREPOEM BOOKS

2012

THE MALADY OF THE CENTURY

JON LEON

FIRST EDITION | FIRST PRINTING

This edition first published in paperback by Futurepoem books
P.O. Box 7687 JAF Station, NY, NY 10116
www.futurepoem.com

Executive Editor: Dan Machlin
Editor/Production: Chris Martin
Managing Editor: Jennifer Tamayo
Other Editors: Ted Dodson

Cover design: Mickel Design (www.mickeldesign.com)
Cover photograph: Kevin Dean (www.betaart.com)

Typesetting: Mary Austin Speaker (www.maryaustinspeaker.com)
Typefaces: Eventide (Cover); Dante (Text)

Printed in the United States of America on acid-free paper

State of the Arts   Futurepoem books is made possible by the New York State Council on the Arts with
the support of Governor Andrew Cuomo and the New York State Legislature, as well as
by individual donors and subscribers. Futurepoem books is the publishing program of
Futurepoem, Inc., a New York State-based 501(c)3 non-profit organization dedicated to
creating a greater public awareness and appreciation of innovative literature.

NYSCA

Distributed to the trade by Small Press Distribution, Berkeley, California
Toll-free number (U.S. only): 800.869.7553
Bay Area / International: 510.524.1668
orders@spdbooks.org
www.spdbooks.org

The author wishes to acknowledge the editors of the following publications and imprints,
in which these poems, sometimes in other versions, first appeared: *Action, Yes*; *Cannibal*;
Fence; *Octopus*; *Soft Targets*; and Solar Luxuriance. "Hit Wave" originally appeared
in 2008 in the chapbook of the same name from Kitchen Press but under the title "1982".

DRAIN YOU

A black God touched me today and I knew I was a poet. When I produce poetry I am responding to a God who touched me in a perverse way. The state of my text is an act of worship to a black female God that told me to worship capital. From a business perspective my poetics is about marketing a God who fondles with my white self. This is what makes my poetry so friendly to the void in the world. I marketed a God who exploits me to bring her message of panic to the poetry sector. I was watching a Kenneth Anger film when a large aphrodisiac God converged on me and told me to create a poem that pleases her. The results of her visit are collected in books called *Hit Wave* and *Right Now the Music and the Life Rule*. The text in these books is to give the audience hope for life today because a black female God told me to.

One of the masterpieces of late 20th century music is "Go Your Own Way" by Fleetwood Mac. This is the song of a lifetime. It explains the point of being in a special way that will blow my mind every time. The break in the middle, created by every thinking man's guitar hero Lindsey Buckingham, is like a high desert or transient hotel. It is totally first. This is the timeless sound of a collective genius, one that will live up to the claim that is Art. Only "Rhiannon" comes close to this pinnacle song, which is also by the band Fleetwood Mac. Only the handicapped would not understand why the album on which this epochal song appeared spent 31 weeks at #1.

I was watching a video of us today and we were so young. We were so ready to be imposed upon. I watched us play guitars and scream. I know you're out there and you want to touch me. I'll let you. Somebody was there who I knew and he was staring into the lens like he was psychic. Our jeans were so torn up but we were happy and we were so high on Colt 45 while we listened to the music that made us fall in love with each other. Living forever is easy in an abandoned warehouse the year punk broke and we drank beer at Neiman Marcus. When it was cold in a storage shed in the middle of nowhere and you worked at a bottling factory.

I know you always loved me for who I am. I fucking miss that. When we are smelling crack from the other room and trashing the motel while we do teenage stuff on the bed. I know that it's just right when we're in the bathroom loving life. I like being a part of this world. I wish we all could be together again and love being alive like we're just walking the streets for no reason. Walking around Chinatown in heels. And we love this life that is never ending. I love it when you gave me the pills at Clermont Lounge on a weeknight. I wanted to puke. The love in the air is so thick and heavy and green. I'm not stupid. I know you are thinking about me and want to call. Do it.

Hanging out at a pool and trying to finger you was so fun. It was a great time. I made you a mixtape. I'm glad you're there. I know you're alive. How does that feel. I'm so numb now. I drive around listening to tapes and thinking about how cool my fantasies are. I look at the French books in the back seat of my car and want to poetry. Did you know that I love to write. I wrote all these sexually charged writings for you. You are my greatest inspiration. Let's hook up in SF. It could be like drinking beer and trying on shoes. Let's go to Edinburgh Castle. I'll do anything with you. I'm really scared.

There's no other way to say this. When you texted me that night outside of the Majestic when we were still being that way and the sun was clean I wanted to tell you the way I felt. I felt like I had ruined our lives. I get so emotional when I watch the same karaoke video of us. Everything about the way people are now is hurting. The way I can be a part of this world is astonishing. I live and you aren't the pieces of my life I've forgotten. When the next song comes on and you are singing remember we did this and we were kings. We ruled.

This year marks stocks' worst start since 1982. I say to myself "This is history in the making" and I pat myself on the back. "You've been a philanthropist too long" Keystone sighs. I walk lugubriously to my home gym. Look at prints of vintage yuppies on the wall. I'm picking titles for my upcoming retrospective and discover an early piece entitled *Portrait of a Nihilist Pornographer.* I'm in luck. I've found my autobiography. Three days later I fly to the City of Angels and meet with Telia. We discuss how insider this book is. Three days after that I'm on a boat called The Dreamliner counting riches with a deformed Brazilian who's chanting "Anything taboo will make me wet." I'm like "This moment is archival."

HIT WAVE

In 1982 Fassbinder died from an overdose of cocaine and sleeping pills. That was the year I was born and New German Cinema dissolved. 17 years later I couldn't make money off art. My personal relationships with people like Ketja and Keystone began to cause severe mental strain. After six years of work the depression was exhausting. The disenfranchised were no longer the heroes of film and literature. The reflection of extreme wealth replaced every image of beauty and abased the very foundations from which our organization sprang. We could either quit or go commercial. Many of our contemporaries in the scene had already accepted that poetry was now industry. Marketing eclipsed the creation of a book and authors were as sycophantic as ever.

The year I was born Saddam Hussein killed 140 men in a town called Dujail for attempting to assassinate him. I mostly listened to Phil Collins and Whitney Houston in the succeeding years. When I was old enough to drive a Chrysler New Yorker I drove stacks of *World News* for InCorp. It marked a political awakening that would remain with me as I attempted to organize an avant coup in 2004. TJ and Keystone, complicit in the insurrection, launched a satellite paper for secular poetry. We sold it on the black market from the back of my New Yorker. Later we bought the black market whole.

The year Versace was killed I was 15 years old. I watched *American Gigolo* on repeat to try and understand. My first short story appeared around that time. A debacle that landed me a heavy fine. To craft the piece I stole several chapters from an out-of-print erotic paperback called *The Cherry Gropers*. Somehow the publishers found me. From that point on I knew that everything I did would be fraught with resistance, would be controversial and incredibly desired – for whatever reason. The commonplace council I received from ordinary individuals was like speaking Dutch to me. I just could not understand their rabble. I drove toward the bright lights.

I bought a hotel building on Liberty Street. We named the place The Commodore. I accepted to allow sixty percent of the rooms residence priority. The whole organization moved in. Around this time the counterculture was bemoaning its loss of all credibility. I went so far left as to prohibit any variation of the dress code in The Commodore. All music was disallowed except what we played through the stereo in every room and hallway. That was mostly Phil Collins. Everyone loved it of course. Fortunately we were still cool, but less neo-bohemian, more Helmsley.

My life until then was a variety of despots: chokehold girlfriends, mindless trysts, naked bodies on a beautiful couch. I hated the way it was constant on top. I knew it to be untrue. Through the media I was in touch with my fame. I excelled under pressure from below. I wrote a book around this time about a dilettante named Sukarov. We were under pressure from the financiers. I abandoned the serial style of the 60s and found the reactionary lyric impossible. An interview in *Doublewide* magazine received over 20,000 hits in the first day. I lied through my teeth but I did invent a new language. "I am a writer" I relentlessly repeated, "I am a writer." But why goddam didn't I feel like it.

I mingled with practicing experimentalists and popular connoisseurs without favor. I moved into a ramshackle studio on St. Charles Avenue, previously a shooting gallery. There I set my Spanish Olivetti typewriter and composed romantic mock-ups and seditious communiqués. My solitary window faced down on an alley and three dumpsters. I slept on a mattress loaned to me by a student at the all girls university. I blew my nights at Lenny's, The Clermont, or MJQ. I gorged my days on masterworks.

Two girls I knew, one a painter and one an obese seductress, began fingering one another in my bedroom the night of the Southcoast Soiree. I had

Keystone remove them from the premises. From the boudoir I could hear my name. I allowed them back into the pool party under the condition they perform atop a float in the water for all to view and possibly participate. Several of my distinguished guests penetrated the couple. I stood by and watched with benign curiosity. Many times I had fucked in groups and was by that time quite disenchanted. Later that evening I was accosted in the street by a gentleman named Ethan. He said to me "You're not really a writer, *I'm* a writer." Then I walked to the newsstand to read the latest reviews of my work.

After a year repairing my debt in a quaint and ridiculous rural town I decided to reach for life and return to Miami. I met a man there who was like a communist Jude Law. We would sit in bars for hours, any time of day or night, and after-hours we'd continue drinking with hairdo strippers and myopic scenesters. I nearly went capitalist around this time but instead went Platinum, Pulitzer, and Palme d'Or. *Tract* was a runaway hit but defiantly unavailable anywhere. My rep suggested scarcity was the perfect soft-hype.

When *Tract* first came out no one could read it for three days. The website hosting the book was overrun with traffic and crashed. This is a true story. I spent the following weeks collecting everything Lynn LeMay had ever done. From a small apartment on East 37th Street in Savannah I began a memoir. Literature was definitely dead, but tabloids were extremely popular, except for *Liaison*, the print version of which had gone under early in the year.

Marcel and I had breakfast at Trieste nearly every day that summer. Late evenings we would drive out to the shore to relax. At those times a melancholic haze covered the sky above the surf. One memorable evening while reading *Mountolive* several seagulls landed near our recliners and I kicked sand at them for some unlocatable reason. At nightfall we'd take the Corvair back to my condo in the Matsonia Gardens building. I'd regularly fall asleep in the nude, recalling a poem from one of my favorite writers: "The Dreams in Your Heart That Never Die."

Through our For the Fans directory we connected with millions of sects throughout the world. Developing nations became a top priority and we found easy listeners in Sudan and North Korea. Around this time I had a surge in income thanks to the theatre applications and barber shop magazines. TJ found a translator who could transmit our communiqués among growing devotees to the east. I made Kasia president of Foreign Relations and repaired my beef with Cameron. He was wildly attractive and had a mind-blowing skill set. Plus he had 2.5 million dollars worth of classic Dutch erotica in escrow, and I was thinking of opening a pleasure palace. Two months later we became the proper recipients. I designed the building in 2003 and had blueprints in a locker at Hartsfield-Jackson. When I finally put it together *Architectural Digest* was there to capture pictures. Cameron's art lined the halls and booths. Ketja and Kasia led the publicity campaign. Keystone acted as procurer. We were all winners.

Many nights in a drunken haze I attempted to seduce avant-class women, most times successfully. A mutual lust in cooperation with the press created a global buzz and inspired a demonstrative cult of personality. To every state in the hemisphere I brought the carousel of life without consequence.

As my prowess increased the attention I received became maddening. I had even thought of telling a slim brunette prostitute she'd be my last lover. I was so anxious about my sudden leap to the top of the game I contemplated suicide. Never in the old days of shoebox flats and cheap brandy would I have thought immediate and deserved success repulsive. To cope I did what any self-stylized man would do. I slung on my car coat and walked like a bullpen expat to the nearest piece of anglotrash.

During the first five years of my career I lived in total squalor. I had been arrested twice and faced multiple charges in different states. The quarrelsome women I had surrounded myself with had all vanished to the margins of society, a caste I had inhabited for as long as I could remember. Somewhat of a petty criminal and drifter I decided that pure beauty must become my new mantra. The old bohemian ways and derelict charm gave way to sartorial pursuits and exquisite eastern landscapes.

I knew that eventually I'd be arrested. Extreme sexual perversions had entered my mind regularly for years. I had managed to restrain myself from committing to any action in this direction with the exception of one fantasy. The recording of these acts committed by others. I used 16mm film to capture two 15-year-old nymphets sucking and fucking a variety of anonymous cocks through a glory hole in my studio. Too excited to refrain I privately screened this masterpiece to an audience of 12. Keystone idiotically invited a stranger who turned out to be a narc from DC. He'd been following my movements since *Body Machine* was released.

I took Keystone's suggestion and met with my attorney in June. The short-run book of vignettes I had written two years earlier was now on the eve of publication and censors were breathing down my neck. There was also speculation in *Poet's Arcade* that I'd be charged with obscenity. My attorney, a slick young Republican with little or no interest in the precocious ambitions of an artistic provocateur, encouraged me to distance myself from the insurgent class. We were planning nothing, had no interest in bombcraft or terrorism, but were considered dangerous to some as we might steal from distributors, hack blogs, and generally fabricate, hoax, and heckle others into uproar. I took his advice, knowing it was in my best interest, and promptly disbanded the Illiterati. For a minute the careerists thought they'd beat me. Little did they expect that I'd come back in one year to disgrace them into humiliation with an essay on transgressive poetics.

"Turn the Music Up and Keep Your Mouth Shut" was invented by Cameron. I met Cameron in St. Thomas with TJ. I did not expect to find a serious German in Yves Saint Laurent drafting an impossible language explaining an invisible environment. But that was Cameron, and he architecturalized our parties. Somewhat of a reformed pederast he still mingled with the sensuous and effeminate. I considered him sweet and he was an undeniable sensation around Georgia. Most of his parties involved soft palettes and advanced assemblages. Our group CounterRev was an impressionistic collage of TJ, Cameron, myself, and Keystone. The sex was better than the best.

To fund my rapidly diminishing market accounts and to fill holes in my international vanguard book collection I regularly worked for and/or published a number of art-class barbershop magazines. These publications graphically depicted full-on female genitalia, less often grainy male genitalia, and appealed to a bleeding-edge heterointellectual market. I returned to 16mm films strictly on principle and began calling them "documentaries" to seduce the big time general audience distributors.

My profession was seedy and distasteful to most. But I was a charming leper, and had enough Strindbergian contempt for the female race to bother seducing them. My new Atlanta comrade was called Tyler and he managed a flawless stag operation. I secured beauties for the screen tests, which were more fulfilling than sestinas. Our first feature was called *Reiner*; our diegesis was called "The Spirit of Whoredoms." I pitied anyone who wasn't me in those perfect times. Following our premier I became *s'occupe des éclairages*. We stopped smoking cigarettes so we could buy more penny stock.

Videotaped Sex resounded as swansong of a debauched, anti-antiseptic minimalist degeneration. I relocated my studio, found magnetic tape loops displaying gaping Indian wench passé, and marched to the fibers of Ketja's nets. She was tirelessly voyeuristic, half-mad, and criminally made up. I watched her struggle as profit margins plummeted and rave effloresced. Though our relationship devalued in the eyes of analysts we took our dog-style predilections straight to the civic association, and secured a multi-figure grant with a breeder of racehorses named Jan. We celebrated with Nina Hagen, Cox Mooney, and a compendium of sophisticated auteurs. Ketja and I had masterminded an underground trade for a nowhere market. *[dot] d.e.* was to be the envy of the minor world. We had regular rooftop benefits.

I met Helen around this time and we decided to rendezvous in Las Vegas. Her bets with the complex dog fighting scene in Oakland and her rap star boyfriend Juan B. were going nowhere. I accepted the conditions of our visit. That is, we had decided to leave gambling to gamblers and drink straight through our four days in the Tropicana. Upon my return to the east I boarded my windows with 2x4's and continued to get high on J&B per usual. My ex was a promoter and regularly invited me to discos and speakeasies. I didn't see light for three months. In a time before hit-offs, breakouts, and aqua-lipped twenty-somethings, I was just a waiter at the Majestic Diner, struggling through drafts of what would become *Kill the*

Father, Fuck the Mother. When this book lifed, Estelle hard-hyped it to #2 in the small press circuit. #2 because my unofficial manuscript *Sequel* was already at #1. *Writing & Culture* wrote an article about me under the headline "Fame Will Make You Free."

I had often joked that ex-poets were the best poets, but now I was discovering it to be startlingly true. Some of the men and women writers showing at the time quipped at my negative prosodic approach to composition. "Fools" I'd laugh. I was the one jet-planing to Stockholm, Vienna, and Melbourne, a stack of vintage *Rodox* on my knee, and reading about myself in the majors. Cameron was exactly right: the best in the land is the richest in the land. After five years I had clearly renaissanced.

Following my ascetic dropout I refugitived to Montsberg. There I was compelled by seductive teenage libertines with eager mouths. As a writer I had achieved an arrogance so profound as to eliminate all possibility of criminal charge. I allowed myself the pleasure that only international prestige can offer. The full and unprohibited availability of total sexual perfection and fulfillment. But I quickly became disenchanted and returned to the work station in February.

A lot of people didn't like me. Most of them were poets. They called me names like proletarian, idealist, romantic, handsome. "Fools" I thought. Why would people sell themselves short and not just live the life of pure creative glamour. It was easy for me, to others it was a mirage. The real geniuses of history were the ones brave enough to be it. I couldn't understand their criticisms to be anything but jealousy. I encouraged their cupidity and became even wilder and more attractive than ever. Around that time I released a book called *Mirage*, dedicated to my detractors. I won't brag about its impact, but it was breathtaking.

Not realizing the gravity of their mistake a little known and unimpressive magazine with the acronym MTD rejected early drafts of my memoir. The editors never returned my queries. I hit up the corner store for a pint of Mad Dog 20/20. Nothing is sacred.

Some of the richer left-front poets of that period made tremendous waves with their revolutionary and investigative praxis. What I couldn't understand in those days was why others and myself, actual workers, were so strenuously ignored. Of course when we spoke of labor, war, or politics, it was not in the voice of high culture and bourgeois education. It sounded more like a palace of knives. I had foolishly imagined all men to be created equal.

Theoretical pursuits were waning. I had lived a sordid existence alongside a German snob with cunt for brains. My old textbooks: *The Butler, Cutlass, FutureMoney*, et al. seemed like relics from a delusional past. New movements, coterie, gallery ultrastructures, and points of interest were released, intellectualized, and just as quickly museumized. The stout German stayed on another two months stomping around the condo while I resigned myself to doleful excursions in my sparsely furnished room. I saw movies regularly but at home I was perpetually annoyed by the passive aggressive kitchen behavior of this *Aperture* reading brat. She even looked at black and white photographs. Luckily, Marcel would visit soon so we could holiday in superior pleasures.

My organization took a night off. 36 continuous months seeking some hybrid of writing and fantasy to publish had worn us down, so we tried to watch *Blade Runner* on a 13" TV. Reenergized by a futuristic nude I'd seen in *Vokna*, we began assembling polypropylene covers enhanced with xerographic hardcore. Usually everyone would pan our efforts.

The underground would do that. Older writers who were younger writers and uncreative creative would criticize most anything we'd innovate. Like conceptual ideas weren't creative. I knew the task was to create something voidish, really nothing. It didn't matter that it was invisible to the general public at that point. Generating press that almost no one would read I found wildly entertaining. Ketja did as well. We did all these performances to introduce the scene to *Golden Slumbers*. I think our maximum audience was 200, but every one of them started their own Economy.

Phil Donahue was the inspiration for many of our imbalanced theatre applications. I found the discussions relevant and did not shy from ripping an episode word for word for the Friday night rehearsals. Every Saturday sold out by dawn. Backstage, Keystone would bring Dom Perignon and wrap-around sunglasses for the performers. We mixed agitprop, erotic dance, and horror to construct a total environment of focused bliss. *Psychedelic Stage* said "The touchable world has no equal." After a successful opening we'd drive my Bonneville around for hours smoking marijuana and rattling our jewelry.

I called TJ in the daytime, always before noon, to discuss with him the prospect of my gems, the possibility of elevating the word poetry to something with a little more suss. He alerted me to the fact that *Poet's Arcade* was calling me "the world's #1 non-academic poet." "Poetry needs more readers and less writers" I told him. He agreed emphatically. Toward the end of our conversation he brought up the distinction between academic cool and world cool. We both agreed that I was world cool. I landed in Arlanda Airport to give my first-ever reading in Stockholm.

When Nightlight was called The Skylight Exchange, GO! was still open, and Raleigh was not the most educated town in America, we'd trade broadsides with the come-uppers. For many years I lived in North Carolina. I sat for my first portraits there, wrote a section which later appeared in *Impulse* to staggering acclaim, and started the first experimental poetry magazine in the New South. But Lyotard welcomed me to the possibility of nothing happening. Later something did happen, but without the rush that comes with being the first boat to dock. It wouldn't be the first time I'd lay the foundation of a thing and later abandon it, but I had romanticized quitting to a maximum. "I hate what I've become" I'd repeat to Ketja, "but nothing can tear me from myself."

At that point I began doing all the things I couldn't do drunk sober. I started with the stock market and quickly launched a refreshing magazine. Nightclubs, interior design, portraits, and eventually cinema would follow. I walked into my studio one night feeling more depressed than ever and said aloud "Make ready for the festival of ruin." Like Jonah sheltered in his whale, I was swallowed up with enough flashbulbs to light up the whole state of New Jersey. *CounterRev* cornered the literary lifestyle market. More famous than cyanide Tylenol, it cost me only $2 to manufacture. Demand would pay $10. Ketja suggested we offshore to Lebanon for even greater profits. Obviously I agreed.

TJ and Brix contacted me from the tower back in Stockholm. I was midway through a self-funded tour. They both got on the line and said "The Hounds of Arawn." I knew what that meant. Stockholm's innovative furniture fair was cancelled due to mobs and riots caused by my latest product. Immediately the dwindling audiences I'd seen the first leg of tour morphed to all out stadium readings. Life couldn't get any more lovable. Annihilation of all feeling overtook me though; the complete madness for my work was so great it was almost corrupt.

It wasn't enough for me to parade others for my own gain any longer. As a young publisher of innovative writing I received more attention than my contributors did. The notoriety is always in the masthead. It is what everyone knows. So I started buying little magazines, shredding away at the fabric of the underground until it was threadbare. The editors could do as they pleased, but as the publisher and the financial wizard behind their existences, I could pull the net from under them at any time. And one sunny day in January that's what I did. Suddenly the entire network disappeared.

"Feel the Real Love" was recorded at Normal Sound for 18 months between vaudevilles in Slovenia and Turkey. Well worth the wait this track alone outsold and outprized Christopher Cross' "Sailing." The B-side, "Training," outsold that. Around this time, what some began titling apex of an era, *Right Now the Music and the Life Rule* bounced 14,700 copies in two weeks. I extended the "limited" label, really just a hype to move books, and reached over 21,000 by the end of the third week. Not bad for a factory-made chap. *Body Machine* was next.

"Songs of Hope" was released the winter before Miami. It quickly outsold Mansfield's "Postcard." Unfortunately I was in Scandinavia doing warehouse specs for our pulp ring. *Analytical Forum* called it "pop under-the-counter . . . atypical brilliance from the only producer that matters." I phoned B. and told her the news. She had already seen it on TV. A record bodega in Kirkwood sold out in 17 minutes.

The pace of life in the days before model theory, graphs, and daily meetings with statisticians chimed regularly with the small bell hinged above the door of the Jackpot members' only club. S. and I were unfailingly available for pints from 8am to 4am and anytime between. Many of my early vignettes began to circulate among the literary junctions from Berlin westward. It was a time of handheld pornography, cool leather, and maniacal passion. But the mythomania surrounding our affairs began to infect and trace with the swiftness of a menacing pandemic. We were blank, and needed desperately to be entertained.

Ghettotech had reached a plateau by the time my dividends accumulated to almost incalculable sums. But the money I had invested in groups like Kasmir, Sims, and Mar-a-Lago disappeared faster than a tube of blow in the offices of the *Miami Herald*. TJ and I initiated a lengthy correspondence regarding what to do at the foot of this cultural aftermath. I suggested St. Thomas, and he agreed.

I wore Florsheim shoes, Levi's 511 jeans, a Christian Dior chemise, trench coat, and aviator sunglasses. I cut my hair with safety scissors, and rarely shaved my face. I smoked Parliament cigarettes, and drank cheap brandy. I lived in Atlanta, Miami, St. Thomas, the Tenderloin, Los Angeles, and wherever else I wanted. I said whatever to whomever.

A fascist at heart, Edward anticipated what would become the Cabratta Club. I put Maxwell in management, and he hired a bevy of Andalusian beauties to waitress, barkeep, and serve in several capacities. Some of our patrons had seen their fortunes multiply exponentially and relied heavily on myself and the Cabratta Club to relieve them from the pressures of single-minded monetary pursuit. I took the job seriously and acquainted myself with a young Tony Curtis-looking fellow named Hathaway, who would eventually publish, and make famous, *French Audition*.

The girls I hung around with at the turn of the century were as into Guess then as they were years earlier at the company's iconic boom in

1982. While writing *Long Hot Summer* in Atlanta I went through a string of glossy women a la Eva Herzigová. Though I lived like a wretch my charisma was irresistible. I remember sitting in a restaurant in East Atlanta Village thinking about a plot error and how Carré sitting across from me looked like Noelle, a girl I met on the terrace at Zane's who said she modeled for Wayne Maser.

My occupations were the effects of a drugged adolescence. Nowhere was this more visible than in my apparel sketches. At the time nothing was new. New wasn't new even and never would be. The pressure was off. Keystone suggested to me that content was an extension of style. So I began to think one-dimensionally. Dream-prole uniforms were the result. I no longer had opinions—ethical, political, or otherwise.

Brix was a serious drinker and a serious thinker. He was also a letch. I let him suck me off once or twice while my girlfriend stuffed her tits in my mouth. At that time I was overwhelmed with declining productivity and found sexual deviousness pleasurably mind-numbing. In the Tenderloin I naively tried to buy marijuana from a crack slinger. After arguing for five minutes at the Matsonia Gardens building gates I threw the bud on the step and slammed the door on him. "Destitute bitch" I thought.

I knew Kalter for ten years before he started the Blanchot syndication, which meant I was there at inception to catapult his early translations to print. He'd foolishly operated a letterpress series of broadsides prior to the Blanchot enterprise. I told him what nonsense it was, that literature was ideas not craft. He got the point that moving forward was better than moving backward. He shaved his beard and rented a hooker angel for TJ and me. Me and her fucked one-on-one maybe ten minutes. Then we just took her by the triples.

Every spring I organized a workers rally, and simultaneously an international film club conference in Moscow. "Not all pictures are made in Hollywood" I'd constantly remind Ketja. Her favorite movie was *Star 80*. At the rallies we drew a surly crowd and listened to speeches by retail cashier Marcel Fuentes. From a discriminating audience not disposed to standing ovations he received three or more year after year. Later, I would lead the crowd into an aggressive "Down with Landlords, Down with the Bosses" pep motto.

I got a ride to Sheremetyevo international airport from someone named Netochka. Moscow rents were skyrocketing so I flew back to the States. The editor of one of the city's longest running underground papers invited me to a small European café in Cabbagetown. We drank wine. I told her the film director she wasn't into was better than the one she was. Later we listened to *Changesonebowie*.

Broadway Video carried exploitation films exclusively. They also provided free condoms at the rental counter. Helen and I visited frequently in the winter months. At that time I lived on the west side with Andrea in a house full of Dalí reproductions and psychedelic paraphernalia. Luckily I was able to move out quickly and lease a studio in Miami. Ketja and I took holiday at the Thunderbird Inn. There I wrote several vignettes under the heading "I Hate American Girls." At night we'd watch the sky turn purple turn pink turn orange-blue and melt into the horizon below the palm trees.

I befriended Keystone early on as a writer. Like me, he had a keen interest in poetry but hated the very word. We decided one night while thumbing the latest installment of *Revue de Poèts* that the problem was surplus. At that time there wasn't much influence to be wielded being a couple of underpublished amateurs, but little by little we managed to shame the pipsqueaks back to the mediocrity from whence they'd come. Anticipating the day when luxury would replace bounty as a prevailing aesthetic.

In abattoir, the momentous gang we'd drafted experienced more success in the first year than in the first five years of circulating clandestine manuscripts. I had taken Cabratta public, I had taken Mar-a-Lago public, I had metamorphosed the very word public. Work became play, and play became pay. Even immediacy was expedited.

"My life is over" I would repeat night after perspiring night. The discos had closed down. My friends nearly deserted me. "Shut it and Lock It, There's a Guy with a Bazooka" bombed in the press and on the charts. Little financial help came from anywhere and my property was forcefully taken away by the courts. Our little slice of pie was now only a plate of crumbs.

In 2003 I couldn't believe I wasn't invited to the single most important event of the year. I felt dumb. I had turned myself from nothing to something and it seemed like no one cared. Right after that I just went and watched commercials and listened to them for a while. I knew I was hot and wanted. Ketja loved me. TJ was my friend. I knew that everyone would be at the huge event of the year and it would be so historical. "But so what" I thought. I was the major star who's absence everybody was asking about. For those people who ignored me everything failed. But I etched their names into my memory as solid as my birth date. Later, the severe sickness and humiliation I inflicted upon them far surpassed their paltry attempts to blot me out. Once the cruelty began their art was obsolete.

By this time, there were huge problems facing me, and I turned from them. I knew that if I faced the huge problems they'd stare me into oblivion. Around the time of TJ's public humiliation as a sideline scab

I decided to come out with my own unpleasantness. I told everyone everything. How I was really the author of *Model Theory*, how I got my start writing press clippings on the Vohm roulette scene, my stint in middle-brow pop outfits, handjobs behind Youngblood, and more. I let everyone know exactly what type of man they were dealing with, and to my surprise their devotion increased.

I wasn't a nice person, nor was I stupid. I invented an *a posteriori* philosophy of magnanimity and betrayal. It was the ultimate provocation and bound others to me more completely. The group of 16 men and women I had selected to monopolize a subsection of the world were of the weakest lot imaginable. I took pleasure in one thought only: that I would eventually lose them in one desperate finale of the basest motive. Yvette's deletion I particularly anticipated. Her hatred for others was presumed upon parenthetical scripts of their very being. She ran a chop shop before meeting me and partnered with the cruelest men ever to adorn a Charvet tie. I could no longer love her alone, nor Ketja. I loved all women and desired them equally.

RIGHT NOW
THE MUSIC
AND
THE LIFE
RULE

Kelley's tits look very natural when she is wearing only a necklace and a heart panty. Her mouth is slightly open. She has black bouncy hair. Her nipples are light. This reminds me of the best things about living life. A pale sun pushes the shadows of leaves onto the wall behind her back. The darts of her eyes are streaked with lace. The jewelry is 15000 USD. The abdomen is wholesome. Everything boring is not worth it. The mood is one of anxious joy. I would smoke a cigarette on the balcony with Kelley. This one is almost as good as the famous photographer who influenced everyone. Habeica can take a picture.

Darla is wearing blue lipstick. She has on blue fingernail polish. Her hair is heat lightning. She reminds me of good times and fun. Her hair is big and black with light curls throughout. Her nose is slim and slightly upturned. She has her left index finger over her lips like "shush." Her eyebrows are black and perfect and her denim jacket matches her makeup. Her earrings are white and her eyes are not very intense but they are urgent. Her teeth are so white I could lick them. I am listening to Eric Burdon as I write this. It is like driving around in a red car through a bunch of palm trees.

Mischa Barton is for bebe. She looks like she is drunk the way she is leaning on the wall. There is a doorway behind her flooded with white light. The wall is green. I can tell that she is sexy by the way her face looks like she will dominate. Her eyes are half-closed and her chin is up. I'm not sure what she is wearing but it is not appealing to me. It is a dress slash shirt with straps and it is purple in color. She is wearing shiny black gloves. Her hair has a wet look. It really does seem like she has been out all night getting wasted.

Asia Argento looks incredibly alluring. The look on her face is like she is in another world. One where perfection and beauty exist only. She is surrounded by 12-inch records and has totally smooth skin and breasts that are barely visible in her Miss Sixty shirt. This shirt is striped with black and red horizontals. Her jeans are very dark and her boots are brown with elevated heels. Basically Asia looks like an alien she is so otherworldly hot. Her hair is framing her face like it is a masterpiece. I am listening to Jens Lekman now.

Lydia Hearst is truly stunning in a dress by Missoni. I cannot describe the dress it is so good. There are rainbow buttons all over it everywhere. She is wearing a top underneath. Her face is stylish and deep. She is wearing a headband that is silky and bronze-brown. This one makes me want to be content and forget politics. It seems like Lydia would like to drink a pale ale and make out hard. I like the background which is illusion. I wish I could see the boots she is wearing by Giuseppe Zanotti.

Mary Woronov has her hand on her head. She is holding a cigarette that looks like it might burn her face. She is altogether mysterious. Unlike the other girls she seems like a real artist. I can tell because her eyebrows are gently raised to a pyramid. I'm not sure what she is wearing because I can only see her head but I know it is cool. She has a delicate mouth and piercing eyes. The ring on her finger is small and just right. The whole picture is like grooving in the fall or winter with some really good friends who are a little bit intellectual, a little bit crazy. I like it.

Katie has sumptuous breasts spilling out of her bra by Agricult. They are arousing and delicious looking. Her face looks exilic and has a just-orgasmed softness to it. Her long curling hair covers one half of an eye. She is wearing a charm around her neck. Her nose is average in a good way and her mouth is tough. She is like someone who didn't do very good in school but is probably a wiz at a number of other more important things. She is lying sideways balanced on her left elbow. Her eyes could make someone nervous.

Ciara is another Elite model. Elite must be the best agency because all the models are from Elite. I cannot see her eyes because she is wearing what looks like very dark ski shades. She has on a pipe cleaner visor and a one-piece swimsuit with a surfing mummy on it. The bangles on her wrist look heavy. She is wearing a see-through plastic-like vest over her swimsuit and posing against white brick. The theme in this photo is like a dream come true. Most of what I can see of her face is her mouth which looks like it would just pucker out and French you if you brushed by it. I think a one-piece is better than a two-piece.

Karen Ambrus is lying down on her back in a Fabucci swimsuit. She is wearing a belt with precious stones on it. Her face is like a cat. Her hair is medium short and blonde and slinky. I am viewing her whole body with silver shoes attached at the feet. Her legs are bent at the knee. This looks like a classic pose and it remains highly effective. This one is more high class, glamorous, and sophisticated. The set is very minimal. Karen's eyes are blue. The whole set-up is timeless and that is what I like about haute couture. This could be anytime.

Elizabeth Taylor is wearing the famous Cartier Love Bracelet. Her breasts are about to spill out of her gown. She has feathers and flowers coming out of her hair. Basically she looks like some kind of mythological type.

Yolanda is smiling. She looks ultimate. Her butt is perky in a pair of short-shorts. She is wearing thigh-high socks. She is in a room that is common looking. Her short-shorts are actually overalls. She looks like she loves life. There is an erotic artwork on the wall next to her. Her hair is red. A shadow crosses her lip. She looks as if she is about to paint herself into memory. Again her ass is lightly tanned and very soft and perky. I imagine she smells like cocoa butter. She is tall and there is an electrical outlet on the wall. She looks very approachable, like she would enjoy a Fanta.

Anonymous Missoni girl is attractive and looks like Vitti or someone. Her hair is garage. The ruby backdrop coalesces with the auto vehicles below my window. Pretty much this one is another 10. She is like Antonioni at his best and is only wearing one item of clothing, a large brown sweater. I see her face forward. She is sliding a hand along the top of her thigh. I would ride with her in a Corvair. Everything is serene. She is at ease in the world but comfortable at home mostly. Because I am an indoors type who is against nature I understand this. I can tell the workmanship is unparalleled. She looks like she has no brains but that doesn't matter. She has an aura.

If you call +1 888 977 1900 you will reach Prada. Prada is going to go public soon I hear and I know their stock will be valuable. Anonymous is wearing a black dress but mostly she is wearing a Prada bag which really jumps out at you. The bag seems like it is almost as big as the girl. I love girls. She is standing against the car and looks disheveled. Her hair is all split up and her face is ghostly, but although she looks like a hooker she remains infinitely desirable. Behind her it looks like a fire is blazing but it could just as easily be city lights. I picture this one at the point abandoned by a young beau. The bag is great. She has dark circles under her eyes. She radiates a gothic sensuality. Everything in the world is permissible and this captures all possibility.

Kelley Devanathan is very provocative when she aims her ass into the sky. It is very white. She is wearing spotted shoes by Christian Dior again. Above her is a lion with his tongue out. The whole picture is risky and fun. Her tits are cushioned by the sofa she is kneeling on. Her eyes are like a female tiger. The pillows are striped red with white in between. I imagine her thighs smell fragrant. She looks entirely content with herself. She looks capable of inviting a man out for an evening. Everything lives.

Isa (while I am listening to *Heroes*). The wide view is pink and red. She is biting keys. For a normal looking person she is attractive. She is wearing a unitard. It would not be difficult to guess who made it. Her breasts spill out into the unitard and are mid-size. She looks like a pretentious one. There is probably a jeep parked outside. The sofa is leather. It is big. Her hair is cut Godard-like like a lot of them these days. All the hideousness of war lies elsewhere. We can forget the world here and yet simultaneously be reminded of it. She has a subconscious bravado. Right now the music and the life rule. She is the real Venus de' Medici.

MIRAGE

DEL RIO

In Chinatown we were wild heart. The dumb sickness of a death. Janáček. Life was so senseless in the boring time. Mostly I was in a labyrinth of icicle pills. The sheepish breasts I pressed my cock between. The way it spurted languidly toward the Tenderloin. I was so crack.

BELLUCCI

I live the life of Stevie Nicks. Orange turn purple hue. I was laid down torpor for the rub. The sadness makes everything impossibly kidish. What if the bouviant chic were holding an exhibition. I know the abstraction is not as good as the vilified dandy. Now I live a sporty life east of the park. We fucked one-on-one maybe 10 minutes before prior objects distracted me.

FAST

My radical body is so really open. View the foot of the bed. Nothing ever changes. Cinema. Time is so hard to imagine. Spiritual wasteland.

FRISCHMANN

I see rivers, parkas on conditioned hair skiers, palm trees across the street. I lay in the tub at the Thunderbird Inn drinking Budweiser. It is so Vietnam-era. To think, 10 years ago, west of Montford, as the moon shallowed.

LIFETIME

I kidnapped a woman. Staring into the abyss. I lived a fag life American.
From the jail I was in I called from the pay telephone. It was like the gulf.
You cartel bitch. Miami was so close I met pasts. Morocco had nothing.
Velvet passengers. I threw women in pools for no reason. Loving a book
by this author. Loving the joy of a watercolor mural painted on the wooden
floor in your Dvořák town palace. I have no fear, I only love the joy. Don't try
to resist the emotions of a lifetime of pure content. Gypsies duel.

THE WAR WILL END

Vox Vivitar Mace. I was born in Japan. A lot of the miscellaneous telephones. I like to drive with the top down. Sure the hair is slick. Still into Armani where I like ruminate darkness. Push you out of a window in red boots. The pussy is the softest.

HARMONY

Nothing ever happens. Except I love my fucking life. Black rain, the very physical environment which turns me. I live in the trance of Aquarius. That is the vision. Maven unto Gods.

GRATIFICATION

Essentially like wine, honey, and roses. The face doesn't look faded it looks attractive. Bronzer, sort of modern. Walking into 37th Street with a packet of fags in my pouch. Leaning into a doorway crowded with women. Everything everything everything.

I AM YOUR VIOLENCE

Reality appears to me. I mutilate it. Cool aura. I cried listening to Cat Power. That which is surrounding. That very name which is time immemorial. Nil Blanche. Dreams, paranoia, static. A signature style which is having, having not.

describe

MIRROR TO MIRROR

Many say it is two or three themes: hookers class war. The same housing project, a bag of weed. When they take the wine-rock whores away. When they find me blacked out under the overpass with a tiny bag of coke. It is a cyclical nightmare. Impulse icon.

When I party it's like I astral project. Fuck nightclubs. At this point I just want to go all the way ditz. I want to invite like 200 strangers to donut my Maserati around a marble statue of a Greek with a trifork. I want to paw endless bottles of sparkling wine and smoke Cubans off the piazza and screen Italian porn out loud in my home gym. Fuck bouncers, fuck security, fuck pat downs, fuck covers, fuck ten-dollar Zima, fuck Uffie remixes, fuck grinding. I want to lick pudding from the fingers of an airhead and throw crystal at the driveway. I want to drive drunk into Brentwood blasting Chicago and hang up on the world. Be a meathead with a mobile phone and a Zilli suit, draining the ATM because it's where the money comes from.

WHITE GIRLS

LISBONS

The way I feel with white girls gives meaning to my life. The way I like to feel the innocent breath of a white girl who is impressed with life and smells like a spa. I cannot resist the touch of essence. When white girls watch me talk to them when we are watching an artistic film and drinking red wine and talking about God's image I feel a tenderness. You want to know my pain. I'll give it to you. I feel like everything is meaningless I say. They are like it is not meaningless Jon and want to give me their bodies. Sometimes I feel like I cannot live without you being obsessed with my face between your legs, because I feel like it's right to make you feel an intellectual feeling between your legs that is not marred by social milieus. When women talk to me and touch me they are meeting me out of time in a place where they exist only. I can make you feel like life has no consequence I say, because I don't have the same attitude of consequence. You want the feeling. I want the feeling like we are able to feel when we first look at each other and we are breaking through to a paperback kind of love making that exists independent of everything. The sweetest voice that asks me to cum on her face. It gives meaning to my life. To meet you at the place in the city when we haven't eaten in many days and are suddenly aware that the light is changing and the world is changing and even our own faces seem to have changed. Looking at each other looking in the mirror thinking about how we look when we are looking at each other. Doing nothing because we want to do everything. Like we are in biographies of great artists. Like you just died in my arms tonight.

FRIENDS FOREVER

On cold and snowy nights I write the most pristine poems for you. I pretend you're in my bed with me and I am touching your thighs, thick and white. And I am pressing my cock between your wet tits. Then I start to heave and have to listen to songs on repeat and think about you like you're an abstraction. I have to escape the pain. I am not cynical enough to stop believing. I know you don't live in Tahiti. I know you are alive and breathing. I know you aren't inside of a film selling newspapers on the street. You are real, clap your hands. You are real enough to imagine you exist next to me. I try to sleep again. I see your face. I try to not sleep, I see your face. I try to drive my sports car, I see your face. I know you aren't only inside of me inside of you. I know you aren't where I left you. I know you aren't in a gravel parking lot outside of a music hall. I know you aren't drunk and texting me. I know you aren't drunk and cheating on me. I need you to appear. I need you to lie down. I need you to lie down in this world in this time. I need you to know the source of all value. It is here. It is in my waterbed.

MY HEART BEAT A LITTLE BIT FASTER

I am young when I lay my eyes on her. She is wearing pleated shorts and a Body Glove shirt. We are lounging at the pool listening to Tom Petty when she slips her hand into my trunks. I am anxious and scared. I think that I feel like kissing hard, making out, but I feel like she wants to do my cock. I am like let's hold each other. She is like uh huh. We are in the showers kissing when I pull on her shorts. I tell her it is right. We will feel like life is a concept, a value. She joins me in masturbating while the Runaways play in the background. I cum warm jets on her white stomach. I am like that is nice. Her purple tank. Her pale face.

THE AURA OF FALSEHOOD

I am not functional without your need to live my cock. I am a slut. I need love. I burn for young girls and women. They don't even have to be white. All over the world there are young girls and women reading my poetry trying to feel my pain. A piece of me is there with them. When I'm alone in my car thinking about the young girls and women, dreaming of their life, I'm thinking about the warm jets. When you are sucking, it is like you are pulling my heart through my dick. When you are bound in electrical cords reading a passage from *Hit Wave* it is my dream. To have you feel ruined by my need to touch this world. Nail my heart to a cross. I am a slut. I am helpless. When I look into a void I see pussy. When I look into the sky I see dark hair, I see pussy. I see you telling me what to do, and me doing it. I see you crying with my cock halfway in your ass. I am crying too. Crying the aura of falsehood.

ALWAY3

On the sundeck at Caesar's picking at a caesar salad thinking the range of world avant-garde experience. Thinking the die is cast, that the desert has touched the sea. Thinking render unto Caesar what is Caesar's, thinking fuck that. Watching the waitress watching the pool, smoking a cigarette, thinking of the waitress thinking about our order. I put my finger on the cleft of my wayfarers and try to hide. Try to hide from the sky. The bathers. We are getting up to enter the hot tub. I'm sitting in the hot tub watching a gigantic television splash images of giant cheetahs and confetti at the ozone. I look at my arm. I look at the checks on my trunks. I try to be real in this moment. I try to imagine a feeling of reality that is authentic and convey that to the surf. I convey that to the surf. Take an Atavan. Talk about the way it is. Look at the American waitress in a blue bikini. In my head I'm thinking what the fuck. I am in a train in East Germany. Feel the grey ghosts of palms in my lap. Feel the sun hit the concrete while I kneel down to pick up a book, put the book on the table. Feel you read the book, with the lights coming up in your eyes.

ARTS & TECHNOLOGY

I like to feel like a Champion. Listening to Frankie Valli say "I can't take my eyes off of you" I feel like New York City is a scale model in my penthouse in North Carolina where I study economics, capital markets, and the World Bank. I like to look into a scene from the top of a building in my hometown down at the traders who are moving here from New York City because New York City started to be kind of like a losing place for wealth creation. Now I look down on them and say to myself "I'm too big to fail." I take my keys off of the ledge and walk down the condominium tower overlooking the entire city. When I reach the parking deck I open the door of a 1980 Mercedes Benz 450 SL and coast to a place called High Street. I'm at High Street knocking back a gin and tonic with three girls I met at the Arts & Technology Center conference on the decline of the book. We have a laugh about the old guard who make a book bound in glue and then pinch angel dust off our palms. At this point I'm so high I'm like, look, why don't we excuse ourselves and go up to my condominium tower I've just invested 3.5 million dollars in. They are like uh, we can do that. So we pile into my 450 SL and ride to the tower listening to the music of Frankie Valli transform our night into a piece of artwork. Nearly there, I look around at the Arts & Technology girls and sort of hum to myself. I feel like I've hit a milestone in my evening when we trip into the foyer of my massive penthouse that has those gleaming glass cubes set into the wall you see in Miami or Miami Beach. From the cubes a glimmer of the prosperity circling this region pierces the dark in the form of an orange-yellow beam of fluorescent light. One of the girls is removing her jewelry and I'm like no, don't. She takes off her clothes instead and lies face down on the carpet. At the stereo I play a song by Frankie Valli. The other two are kind of standing around surprised, I think, by the curtain of paperback books lining the north wall. Those are only bound books I tell them while I finger the Kindle on my coffee table. It is the new large Kindle and we are looking at a book called *Boredom* by Alberto Moravia, taking turns reading passages from the screen. When we get to the part when the boho girl is fucking the protagonist the totally white breast of one of the Arts & Technology girls slips coolly from her blouse. Pretending not to notice I continue to read in my turn. The girl sitting on the other side of me is wearing some totally white string of pearls and she's removing everything but the pearls. I continue to read the screen while the Arts & Technology girls start to make out like I had been planning for them to do ever since we licked angel dust off each other's palms. I get up and go to the stereo, set the needle back to the gold record "Can't Take My Eyes Off You," and walk calmly to the sofa. Once I'm there I melt into the sand-rubbed upholstery with the Arts & Technology girls who haven't yet passed out on the floor. While I'm lying with my back to the armrest I glimpse a piece of sky I've seen only in films of the old grain. It's a wild purple darkness with a bright white hole in it. I'm thinking to myself God, my personal Jesus Christ and saviour, I want you to come down here through that hole in the night and join me in Eden.

SO YOUNG

I am with three or four girls from a place that is like a gloss and we are looking at this part of Los Angeles that is like a bulb. Everything is large and I am looking by myself into a place beyond the world just beyond the air. I am on that side of the air that people refer to in horoscopes. I am able to look into a piece that is broken in the essence of the world. I know what the world is because it is liquid. I didn't give up on the essences. We are looking into a perfume bottle so intently in this gentrified part of town and we are like my god this perfume is so poison. We are watching a sexual videotape that is digital. We are looking into the ground of a parking lot and inside of it are bachelors. Several bachelors emerge wearing tight black jeans and they are putting their hands on the fire rockets inside of the air inside of the world. We are like looking into each other and seeing a Brian Jones type of world where Gods are free to live inside of Gods. I casually take my hand out of its resting place. I say nothing, just stare into a picture. I feel like sometimes the world is like a picture that moves. Like another mpeg it is worth it to ask yourself what is the meaning of life. Do you think life is real I ask one of the girls. They are like uh. I am like this is not anything that is happening it is a picture of nothing else. I go into the burbs listening to the sunbeams in my living room while listening to the music of Shostakovich. I feel like saying yes to everything. I have just adopted a 16-year-old foster nymph. We are banging in the greenhouse. It is a puce moment.

WT

LA ISLA BONITA

I'm with four or five people on an elevator with a glass door overlooking the entire ocean that hovers above a ruined city like an Egyptian stela carved into the wall of the air. I'm wearing Surface To Air denim and patent leather Florsheims. Everybody else looks dimpled. I think I shouldn't text you this. I text you this. Standing on the rail looking at a panoramic plaque with three girls I picked up at Wasteland. I did them both not five minutes ago with Rick in the changing room. Jenny Kayne shorts, Body Glove T-shirt. Came hard on her extensions. I'm thinking this as I step off the elevator into a crowd of minaret dancers faux-banging each other on the marble floor between a circular glass buffet. It's not an actual club but I hang around until Marla beeps me. Marla beeps me. I call her back from a payphone on the hotel balcony. Tell her I saw five blondes peel a banana backwards from the foot of my satin sheets. I tell her I'm a part of this. Are you a part of this.

ADULTS ONLY

They call me an American poetry bad boy. The groupie of the grotesque. Because I move like a mist, seeking the border that seeks to contain me. I stand at a metro platform, my life's possessions in a bag the size of an attaché, and catch the blowback of a life encased in the tyranny of pulp. A pulp novel called *Soft Thighs* written for adults only in the year of the stag. I throw down the book and finger the tear in my lamb's wool sweater. The sweater that smells like the jade room at a Korean spa, like an ambience of finery worn by the whole of the zeitgeist.

This book was set in Dante, the last and most successful typeface designed by Giovanni Mardersteig, founder of the printing houses Officina Bodoni and Stamperia Valdónega. Mardersteig designed Dante for the letterpress, and the metal letterforms were cut by the great punch-cutter Charles Malin. The typeface was first used in 1955 to print an edition of Giovanni Boccaccio's *Tratello in Laude di Dante*, after which the the typeface was named. Mardersteig worked with the Monotype foundry to develop a machine-set version of Dante, and Monotype later developed a digital version, revamped in the 1990s to more closely resemble Mardersteig's originals.